Sharing Heaven With Mom

Sharing Heaven With Mom

A son discusses his near-death experience with his 90-year-old mother and what it means about this life and beyond.

Steven Dobbie, Ph.D.

Steven Dobbie has asserted his right to be identified as the author of this work in accordance with the Copyright Designs and Patents Act 1988.

This work is a true story of the author. For privacy reasons, some names, locations, and dates may have been withheld. Any resemblance to other stories, true or fictional, persons, living or dead, is entirely coincidental. The images used in this book, including the cover, are not the actual places or people described in the book. Do not attribute the content or views expressed either implicitly or explicitly in the book with any people or places in the images.

Please note, you should not read or continue reading this book if you have thoughts of depression or suicide and should instead seek medical help.

After reading this book, if you are interested in learning more about the author and his mother and information about launches of follow-on books then please visit:

www.sharingheavenwithmom.org

DEDICATION

To mom, who brought me life and provided a safe, loving, and nurturing environment for my mind, body, and spirit.

I hope this book brings you great pleasure and eases your mind about the future.

TABLE OF CONTENTS

ACKNOWLEDGMENTS

First and foremost, thank you, mom, for listening to me read this book to you and for providing your thoughts. It has been a wonderful experience, deepened our connection, and provided us with lots to talk about.

Special thanks to Erika, my wife, for her invaluable help, patience, and understanding throughout the writing and publishing of this book. I know I can always rely on her sound judgement.

Thanks to the support and encouragement of my local writers' club, including Andrew, Chris, Bill, Cathy, and many others.

Special thanks to Andrew Sparke of APS Publications for his invaluable advice on all aspects of publishing.

Thanks to my wider family for reading the drafts and providing helpful comments.

Thanks to special friends Dr Marieanne Leong and Professor Satyajit Ghosh, for their reading of drafts and comments on the book cover design.

Finally, thanks to Mrs. Smith for going the extra mile as a teacher.

APÉRITIF

Mom, this book is for your 90th birthday. May you live to well over 100 years old in good health! You don't know this yet—since almost nobody does—but I had a near-death experience when I was younger, and since then a lifetime of thinking and learning about what life is, seeking to make sense of our time on earth, and reflecting on what happens to us when we die. I have put this book together to share my thoughts and experiences and to discuss them with you. I really hope you will find it comforting as you navigate your senior years.

When I began writing the first chapter, I thought I could make it more appealing if I named the chapter an 'appetizer', rather than an 'introduction', as I know how much you love food! This inspired me to write the book with a structure that paralleled fine dining. I know this sounds rather unusual as it's not about food at all, but in a similar way I want you to sample a set of distinct ideas and experiences from my life one-after-another in just the same way that you would experience fine dining as a sequence of dishes that builds flavors towards an overall experience. So, each course is usually one thought, experience, or reflection, constructed as delicately as I could to provide you with a unique overall experience. In keeping with fine dining, each course will be introduced by a server, which will be me.

After reading each course to you, I will distil your comments from our discussion into a response, and I will include it at the end of most courses (chapters). I hope you enjoy the playful dining format. More importantly, I hope this book provides you with interesting insights and meaning, but I especially hope it provides you with comfort and a way to approach death when it eventually comes.

Bon appétit,

with love, your son

Mom, your table is ready. Please come through to the dining room to be seated. Our finest table is ready for you!

Photo credit: liudmilachernetska on 123rf.

HORS D'OEUVRES COURSE

Mom, in keeping with the dining format, I will introduce this course. In this course, I want to share with you about my first thoughts on death. This will take us both back in time and get us thinking about the subject, and it may draw up some of your own memories. People seldom talk about death, even though it shouldn't be such a taboo subject.

Enjoy this first course, mom, and I'll collect your thoughts once you've had a chance to absorb the course and I've discussed it with you. As mentioned, I'll present a summary of your main thoughts at the end of the course and then I'll return to introduce the next course.

As a child, I vividly recall the first time I realized that someday in the future I would die. There was a series of nights in bed when everything was quiet and dark.

My busy day of playing had ceased, and I had time to ponder. Why I started thinking about death, I don't know. Perhaps it was mentioned to me by one of my older sisters. However, I very clearly remember being in bed and I was sobbing from the thought that at some point in the future I would cease to exist, forever! This was like a first awakening for me, to come to know that my time on earth is finite.

Moments like this change how you value your life in a fundamental way that isn't fully realized until many years later. In bed, I was imagining far off into the future when I would die and the last moments and thoughts I would have. I visualized my death very clearly and it was a mixture of dread, fear, and sadness. There wasn't anything good about it really, no 'upside' at all. The worst bit, it seemed, was that I would have to go through it on my own. Sure, your loved ones could be there, but they wouldn't be going through it at the same time.

Mom, you came into my room and talked through my fears and gave me a big hug. I had many questions,

and you quickly knew you were in for a difficult time, but what could you say when your child asks, 'will I die?' or 'what happens to me after I die?' I was

Photo credit: trgowanlock on 123rf

aware and sensitive enough to know the truth about mortality, but too young to properly deal with it. I recall you bravely tried to address my worries in many ways, and you eventually realized there was traction when you told me that I didn't have to worry about it right now. You said, it was a long, long way off, and I had my whole life to live before I had to think about it again. It really was testament to your positive, keep-moving-forward approach that I've seen evident throughout your life. I am sure your positive attitude has contributed to you living into your nineties, with hopefully many more years to come.

My death being a long way off into the future took the pressure off. It made sense to me, and it made my fear a lot more manageable, but it didn't take away from the fact that I would die. There is no unlearning that! There were no magic adult's words that could explain all this away, like some secret explanation that only the adults knew and weren't saying. In fact, it is a hidden truth that most adults avoid if they can, and I'd just happened to come upon it at a very young age.

I have an inquisitive, sensitive mind, so when you left the room after easing my concerns, I thought about death again in greater detail. I imagined what my last moments would be like, literally moment-by-moment. I imagined the fear I would have when death was literally in the next second. I pictured my death happening, and then nothing, forever! I also thought about all my family, including dad and my sisters all

3

dying. It all sent me into tears many more times for a few more nights, but, somehow, I managed to muffle my crying sounds, since I knew there wasn't anything more parents or anyone else could explain, and that felt strange. I had, as a child, stumbled upon the boundary of adult knowledge and reached an impasse that adults couldn't explain away. Anyway, I had a grim clarity for now, but at least I was assured it was a long way off in the future.

Preamble to mom's response

I hope that wasn't too difficult to hear, mom. There really isn't anything more you could have said or done better.

As you know, my plan is to read each chapter to you and then get your thoughts. We've had a discussion now and I've gathered your main thoughts and I've summarised them below.

Mom's response to the Hors d'Oeuvres Course

I was deeply saddened that you were going through this. You were such an intuitive child. A real deep thinker and most kids don't realise about such things or think them through like you did, and the effects on others. We are all different and most kids just go through childhood happy-go-lucky not thinking of such things.

Back when I was consoling you as a child, it was difficult, as I had hoped to give you a really good answer that would help guide you for the rest of your life. Although, I didn't feel like I gave you the perfect answer that would completely satisfy you. So, it was difficult, but I knew I'd be there for you to chat more, as needed.

AMUSE-BOUCHE COURSE

I hope the last course wasn't too difficult for you, mom. Parents always want to relieve their kids of worries, but this is one of those instances when it isn't fully possible. For the next course, as the title suggests, it is meant to amuse you. It may appear a little frightening at first, but rest assured it will end well. The intention is that it will give you a snapshot into the fascinating inner workings of the mind. Grab your blanket and hold tight! Enjoy.

Around about the same time as my thoughts of death, I was lying in bed one night with my head on the pillow, in the quiet. I heard footsteps of someone... or something! I wasn't sure where the sound was coming from. Was it from within my room? I turned on my sidelamp, and I looked around but saw nothing. I then gathered up the courage, whilst lying in bed, to whip my head down under the mattress to look under the bed. Not a desirable thing to do as a child under the circumstances, but thankfully there was nothing there. Was the sound coming from the hallway? I opened the door a crack and looked out into the hall and nothing there either. So back to my bed with the wonder of where the sound was coming from. Strangely, it didn't feel like it was from this world at all! It felt like the sound was coming from within me, to be honest!

The sound was terrible. It sounded to me like it was something stepping upwards on cold concrete steps one-at-a-time in a very heavy-footed way! Fear started to set in... Whatever it was it seemed very cold, deep, distant, and creepily unrelenting! It just kept coming up

Photo credit: membio on 123rf

those steps, slowly but surely, one-at-a-time. I started thinking about what would happen when that 'creature of the deep' reached me! It was a long way down those stairs, but if it did reach the top then what would it do to me? I thought it would likely kill me since it was a terrifying creature indeed.

Reflecting on the 'monster from the deep' in later years, I realized that the subconscious had 'stepped into action' realizing that I was unable to fully handle the thoughts of death I was having at the time. Consequently, it served up this distraction of the 'monster of the deep' to take my mind off the impasse I had reached about death. Of course, the fear I had about the monster was linked with the fear I was having about dying. The subconscious skillfully linked the two and distracted me with the more pressing monster situation. The subconscious knew there were unresolved feelings and learnings linked to my thoughts on death that needed to be resolved and understood later.

The monster was, however, a much more pressing threat, and it certainly distracted my attention from previous thoughts of dying in old age, that's for sure! This monster was poised to kill me much sooner. In some strange way, though, it was less scary since it was uncertain whether it would actually kill me or not. It all depended on where that monster would emerge at the top of those stairs!

It was a lot to handle, and I recall explaining about the stepping sounds to you, mom, and my sisters to get everyone's views. It was very difficult to explain as I couldn't even explain where the sounds were coming from! After a few confused faces, my dad returned home later and was tasked with listening to my explanation and hopefully making sense of it. After listening intently and thinking it through, he questioned me further and predicted I was likely hearing the pulse in my ear on my pillow. After some experimentation, I realized he was right. Thank goodness! He was correct!

Photo credit: romrodinka on 123rf

I was hearing my pulse in my ear when my head was buried in my pillow, and all was quiet. It was such a great relief! It even explained the hastening of the monster when my heartrate increased with fear!

So, the subconscious had beautifully patterned this

monster into my thoughts with what was unique in the environment at the time as I was lying in bed thinking about aging and dying. Unique at the time was the thump, thump, thump of my heartrate, so it linked that with the sound of the stepping of the 'monster of the deep'. Whether intentionally or not, it had successfully distracted me.

Very interestingly, when this issue of the monster was resolved, the subconscious was satisfied that I'd resolved the issue of death as well, at least for the time being. I was free to be a child again without any worries; however, unbeknownst to me it likely sparked a lifelong journey to understand this world and our place in it.

Aside from temporarily resolving my concerns of death, you may be wondering what else I took from the experience. Well, I learned that the subconscious is there to support our lives the best it can. I view the subconscious as an assistant that helps to track important events like, for example, thoughts and emotions about dying for later consideration. It does this in addition to a vast array of other tasks such as ensuring your survival, storing and retrieving memories, giving you reminders, running your body, and innumerable other things.

You must be careful, though, the subconscious is only the assistant and a complex and powerful one at that. It provides thoughts to your awareness for consideration that aim to support you. However, the essence of 'you' is your awareness within, which is separate to all these thoughts. It is the 'you' within that does the perceiving of this world. The essence of me didn't manufacture the 'monster of the deep', it was presented to me. It's very important to make this distinction between what is presented to you and 'you' as your essence that does the perceiving.

Preamble to mom's response

I realise upon reading this to you that it is another difficult one for you to hear, mom. Sorry to put you through hearing about the 'monster of the deep'. I'm sure it is not easy listening; to hear your child struggling with thoughts of death and monsters. Below, I've summarised what you said from our discussion.

Mom's response to the Amuse-Bouche Course

It really must have been terrifying for you to go through this, and I figured this would come up in the book. It was a lot to handle for such a young little boy. I recall you talking to us about the monster, and you didn't know what was happening. I didn't know what to say. We thought it might be a bad dream, and I was so glad when your father figured it out. You seemed fine the day after, so I was relieved. The mind can run away with too much thinking, and you certainly thought a lot as a child. I just wanted all my kids to feel safe and happy, and this worried me since it made me think that you might not be feeling that way. The monster makes sense, and it wasn't by chance that it came about and helped in the way it did.

SOUP COURSE

Mom, have you ever had an experience that gave you a hint of something beyond this world? Beyond what you experience in normal life. In this course, I'll share with you just that. The world beyond our normal life is around us all the time, but it is usually ignored or not even noticed.

I know you are eager to hear about the near-death experience, but don't worry, it will begin soon enough. First, I want you to hear about some other experiences that might provoke your own thoughts and experiences about the world beyond. Enjoy!

As an adult many years later, my wife and I moved to England. I was driving home alone from work one afternoon. For me, the drivetime is a time to relax and just let my mind wander freely and discard all the thoughts of the workday. This was one of those casual days when I was enjoying driving through the English countryside of rolling hills and meandering narrow roads and field-after-field of lush green shrubs and trees. The green fields were dotted with patches of trees, sometimes beautifully arched right over the road and you can drive right under them. On the route home, the road dips into a small valley, winds around a bend, and then ascends the opposite side. You need to pay particular attention through this section, or you'll run right off the road.

One particular day, I was just focused on the road and letting my mind wander to whatever came. After I maneuvered the dip in the road and had driven under the dark cover of trees and was ascending the other side of the tree-lined valley, I had a beautiful experience. I momentarily glanced to the left looking through a gap in the trees and saw a striking view of a bright sunlit yellow field.

The field was incredibly yellow and contrasted spectacularly with the surrounding green fields and the dark shade I was driving under. Now, you might have seen yellow rapeseed fields like this before, but this was the first time I had ever seen one so vibrantly yellow with the sunlight shining brightly and contrasting with the dark shade I was driving under. With only green fields all around, I was momentarily shocked and stunned by the view. The color of the field and how it contrasted with the shade was surreal. Crucially, the bright yellow field was far-too-far for me to see the individual rapeseed plants, so it looked like the landscape was literally painted bright yellow, with the yellow covering the land part-way down into the valley. Although my glimpse was only for a few seconds, all my thoughts were instantly emptied, and it was as if my brain had tried to make sense of the yellow painted land but couldn't. I was left absorbing the scenery in pure awareness, completely without a thought. It was like the subconscious and conscious were both mesmerized and stumped at the same time.

When the mind-body becomes aware of something unusual and striking, then it can seem very special; but, when it is truly caught off-guard, then you are left with a blank conscious and subconscious that have nothing in response and are temporarily shut down—no anticipation, no processing, nothing at all. The mind/body are completely stopped. What triggers this experience is unique to each person and a trigger for one person is unlikely to trigger for another person. Even for the same person, a trigger is unlikely to be a trigger again. Some people refer to these experiences as satori moments—momentary enlightenment.

What you are left with is a pure awareness of reality without the clutter of the mind and body. I would say that in that moment you are experiencing your pure spirit that is always there but is just normally the quiet observer of your life. It's as though you lose all experience of yourself and your mind processes. You experience the reality of the moment without any of the dressings of life. This experience can be triggered by a multitude of things in the world including natural and manmade, but it is rare. It isn't so much about what you are looking at, but more about it surprising you and causing you to experience from your essence, your spirit.

It feels like you are at one with whatever triggered the moment, but it's also important that you don't get too caught up with what triggered the experience. What you have viewed isn't special beyond triggering the moment—it is still mundane. It may trigger for you and not for others. It is usually uniquely personal. It may be beautiful like a sunset, for instance, or it may be more mundane. What is common is that it surprises your mind processes into temporarily ceasing. This is unique and can allow you to experience your inner spirit— which is really very special.

This inner spirit which you perceive from is what I call the 'spirit awareness', since you are perceiving from your spirit essence through your human body and the associated senses the body provides. I will distinguish this from your full spirit after I first describe my near-death experience. I believe everyone has access to the spirit awareness through their perceptions. It is subtle and seemingly insignificant, though, which is why most people overlook it. But rest assured it is there and it is the essence of you experiencing the world right now and for all your life. As a scientist, I don't see any way of measuring the spirit within. It is beyond the physical, and I haven't seen any convincing evidence that it is just the workings of the brain.

So, what prevents us from experiencing the 'spirit within' all the time? Well, it is things that distract your awareness. I call them obscurations since they obscure what you see. Obscurations are the distractions by the mind and body. For example, thoughts that take you off in various directions, such as reminders you think about, songs you hum, or bodily sensations that distract you, etc. If you can dampen down these obscurations then you can experience your essence, your spirit, right now.

Meditation helps you to do this. If practiced over time, it can quieten the mind/body enough to allow you to see what is always beneath. To quieten the obscurations, or at least not be distracted by them, is far more difficult than you might think, however. The mind, body, and your environment tend to clutter and obscure your perceptions even though they are essential for you to initially become aware of your spirit (I will explain this later).

Unfortunately, mind/body obscurations incessantly distract you from your spirit through urges, desires, wants, thoughts, emotions, etc. So, for most people they get very little or no time at all to recognize their spirit. Keep in mind, I am only suggesting that obscurations are detrimental to *realizing* your spirit. Once your spirit is recognized sufficiently, then indulging in obscurations (especially thoughts and emotions needed for everyday life) for most purposes is fine and essential for living. You don't want to have to exist in a meditative state away from the world for your whole life! When you understand you are, in essence, something more than just the physical and mental aspects of you, then you can develop the spirit within you. This brings great peace to your life and is also valuable preparation for passing.

Most people ignore the spirit within as insignificant gaps between thoughts because it is subtle and quiet, and seemingly unimportant. But, mom, I want you to be aware of those gaps and, even better, meditate and settle the mind/body down and become aware of what is there when you are not thinking, feeling, or doing anything. Even doing this regularly for very short periods is beneficial. Over time, you will begin to recognize your spirit in those gaps between thoughts, actions, feelings, and distractions, and eventually you'll experience from your spirit essence even in everyday life away from meditation.

Preamble to mom's response

Mom, this was a very different course to the last two since it focused more on recognising the spirit and what clutters up the perception of it. It was lovely to read this to you and chat about your personal experiences and thoughts. Below, I've summarised the essence of what you said in our discussion.

20

Mom's response to the Soup Course

I loved reading this chapter, especially hearing about your driving home as you sounded happy and content. I can relate to your story of the field because I have had an experience like this, but I didn't realise the significance of it until reading this chapter. Very true about the obscurations getting in the way of recognising the spirit.

APPETIZER COURSE

Some experiences in life let us know very concretely that there is something beyond this world that we do not fully understand. In the next couple of courses, I will share some very private experiences that I've not shared with many others.

Why share them now? Well, mom, you are 90 years old and I know from our chats that you are thinking about the big questions of life, death, and meaning. In addition, there is also worry about you catching Covid-19 which has really pushed me to write this book as quickly as possible. My aim was to write down my experiences in this book to give to you in the hope that it will bring you greater peacefulness in your latter years. This next experience is spread over two courses. In this course, I will set the stage for the first experience, and then I will go into full detail and complete it in the next course. Thus, I will hold off reporting your response until the end of the next course. Enjoy.

I was met with a very difficult decision. Dad's health had taken a turn for the worse and it wasn't clear how long he would live. He could potentially survive for up to six months in the state he was in, but he could pass as soon as a couple of weeks; the doctor was very unsure. The decision I had was to fly back home to see him now before he died or delay and try to 'time' a trip so that I saw him just before passing and could attend his funeral. Living and working on a different continent is very challenging at times. It was a very difficult choice, but I chose to return home immediately and see him for what was likely to be the last time.

I had to go to the embassy to get my passport last minute, as it had expired, but all that worked out as smoothly as possible. I took the next flight and was met upon landing at the airport by one of my sisters. She took me straight to the hospital as she was due to visit him that day. She said I could stay alone with him all day and have some special time since I had just returned from overseas. I hadn't seen dad in many months, nor any of my family in Canada. My sister warned me that he couldn't really communicate by speaking much anymore, so it was a significant change to be prepared for, but she said that he still had some energy and emotions in short bursts.

We arrived at the hospital. Dad had certainly aged, and indeed he couldn't even get words out very well now, but I could tell he was still fully present and interacting well. My sister could still understand most of what he was trying to say, but it was difficult for me. I recall just months before having dinner with him and he was full of life and still had lots of energy and vim. Now, he was limited to being able to communicate with facial expressions and some muffled words.

From his expressions and gestures, he was overjoyed to see me, and we had a very emotional chat which I treasure as much now as I did back then.

My sister said he was getting tired more frequently in recent days, but said he perked

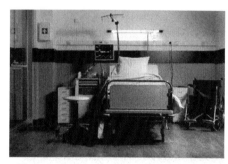

Photo credit: dragoscondrea on 123rf

up and had a lot of energy upon seeing me. He was certainly happy and emotional. My sister left to give me one-to-one time with him, and I spent the whole day there at his hospital bedside talking to him about his life experiences. As I knew his more recent memories were likely faded, I focused on his older memories. I talked with him right the way through all his main life stories in chronological order. I knew his stories well because we spent considerable time travelling together in a car when we previously worked together.

I could tell he was so overjoyed to relive his key memories of growing up in Scotland, going to the local grammar school, his relationship with his grandmother, the friends he had, getting called up for the second world war when he was playing golf, struggling hard to study during the war to earn his officer classification, etc. He tried to communicate several things, but it was difficult. From his facial expressions, I could tell he was deeply emotional about my being there and it was a great joy for us to share that very special time together. I could tell he was trying to tell me things and you just know instinctively what those things are.

It was very difficult; I recall going to the hospital cafeteria alone for a coffee and some food in the middle of the day and just being in tears the whole time. Curiously, I was glad nobody tried to comfort me; I just knew it was natural to experience. Back in the room, we spent the rest of the day going through more of his memories. It was a very special connection we had that day. When someone is towards the end of their life, if they have peace of mind then they focus on what is important. The connection is very deep and genuine. It is unfortunate he couldn't verbalize, though, but I knew what he was thinking about. My sister returned. We were due to go back to her home, get settled in, and have dinner with more of the family. I told dad that I'd be around for a couple of weeks and so we would have a lot more time to chat.

That night at my sister's home, we had a wonderful dinner around lots of family and it was just lovely. We enjoyed the night and then we all retired to our bedrooms and fully expected to sleep the night through.

Mom's response will come at the end of the next course, as these two courses are strongly linked.

SALAD COURSE

As mentioned, this continues from the last course. Mom, I hope you are ready for this course. Things are about to get a whole lot more interesting. Mom, your comments will appear at the end of this course. Enjoy.

Upon retiring to bed, I found myself to be very tired, as I had an emotional day with my dad and a wonderful evening with family. I slept for hours but then suddenly awakened. It was the middle of the night and was still very dark and quiet. I was awake but only slightly and my mind had not started spinning up thoughts yet. I was in that state that inventors keep the pad of paper at the side of their bed for, things come.

I was halfway in a dream-like state and became aware of being in a store. I was browsing and looking at unimportant items on a tall metal stand that squeaked when rotated and had little knick-knacks hanging all over it. Suddenly, I started moving backwards, like I was sliding, yet I wasn't moving a limb. I couldn't resist it either. I continued backwards like a ghost slowly going through the shelves behind me without them crashing down around, or even moving at all! It was surreal, and strangely nobody else shopping in the store took any notice. I continued backwards through a big glass window until I was outside looking in at a modern store with large glass windows from floor to ceiling. I could see people inside still browsing around shopping. It's like I was dreaming but I was in an awake state.

Something then caught my attention in the night sky just above the store. It was like a shooting star! It was

progressing slowly but steadily upwards in the night sky. It was glowing brightly with a glistening trail behind it. At first, I was just fascinated and mesmerized by the beauty of it.

Photo credit: composite photo with building by brandonkleinvideo on 123rf and sky by author

I was in a state of spirit awareness observing it.

Suddenly, it dawned on me with every inch of my body, that I was looking at my dad's spirit ascending and leaving this world. I watched as his spirit continued its journey upwards and then disappeared and was gone. I knew my dad had just passed! It wasn't just that he had died that was so captivating, it was also that I had literally just been watching his spirit leave this world!

I jumped out of bed and flicked on the light. What should I do now? It was the middle of the night. How could I explain this to my sister? How could I wake her up and say what I'd seen? I spent some time thinking about it all and wondering what to do next. It's a strange feeling to know with every inch of you that something had happened, yet you have no external proof of it. On one hand, I felt brimming over with the excitement that I'd experienced this 'marvel' of seeing my dad's transitioning spirit going beyond this world. On the other hand, a feeling of deep sadness that I was sure I'd just lost my dad. I needed verification.

Soon after, the house telephone downstairs began to ring. It was the middle of the night, so it was very unusual. I leapt to the bedroom door, opened it, and zipped into the hallway. I stood there waiting for someone to appear as I listened to the phone downstairs ringing again and again. I was ready; it all made perfect sense. It rang several times and then my brother-in-law came out of his room and went downstairs. I waited with bated breath, but he returned upstairs and nonchalantly said it was a wrong number and disappeared off back to bed.

What! How could it be? From the hallway, I returned to the bedroom bewildered and deflated. I recall pacing around the room thinking that the universe had never seemed so out of its natural order. I got out my pad of paper and I wrote down everything that had occurred to me that night, especially about seeing my dad's spirit ascending.

Shortly after I'd finished writing, the phone rang again, and it just felt right, like the universe was back in order again! I shot back into the hallway. I knew it was the hospital, and it was. Certainly, a mixture of feelings washed over me about the loss of my father, of course, but also the fact that there is far more to this world than meets the eye. As expected, they informed us that my dad had recently passed.

I really wish I had gone downstairs and picked up that first call! Also, I wish I had put 'pen to paper' and written this book years ago to give to my dad before he passed.

Preamble to mom's response

Mom, the world is certainly a more complex place than it appears. The spirit world is around us all the time and, circumstances permitting, you can tune into it, but most of the time we don't even notice it at all. Below, I've summarised the key points of what you said in our discussion.

Mom's response to the Salad Course

I've enjoyed these two courses. The introduction to the Appetizer course is so sweet about your hope to bring greater peacefulness! I loved reading that.

Well, you had a premonition and saw it through. That is incredible! I've learned a lot from listening to these courses. You must be open to this sort of thing. It's unusual but your life will be interesting because of this ability. Embrace it! I'm also glad you had time to spend with your dad in hospital and that it was so emotional.

FISH COURSE

Well mom, this is what you've been waiting for. It's time to read through my near-death experience. I have split this experience over two courses again since it would be a lot to read and discuss in one night. I'll set the context for the near-death experience in this course and in the next course I'll walk you moment-by-moment through the near-death experience. Grab your pillow for comfort as these courses will again be difficult to hear! I will gather your comments and present them at the end of the next course. Enjoy.

One beautiful sunny summer's day, my friends and I took a long drive to a beautiful nature-spot. After walking a little way, we came upon a gorge nestled in the trees. Yet, we couldn't see it fully at first since the trees obscured the view. But we were all excited and descended into the gorge through the trees jogging down the slope within the forest. It was gently sloping at first and had a light and airy feeling about it. Within the forest, you could see all the towering trees with branches and leaves way up overhead giving a feeling of being in nature's cathedral.

We couldn't see the bottom of the gorge yet, so we kept on moving, but we could hear the power of the water going over the waterfall and hitting the base of the gorge down below to our left. The pounding of the water sounded so heavy, like the deep rumbling of a train. We couldn't go directly down the side of the gorge to the waterfall, as it was too steep, so we took a gentler route down. We were eager to get down there, though, sometimes following the path and sometimes not, sometimes running, sometimes not. The brilliant summer sun was beaming through the trees here and there, and we were all excited and knew it was going to be a perfect day.

We finally emerged at the base of the waterfall and made our way over to the side of the falls and even ventured somewhat behind it whilst trying not to get too wet. The rocks had a green slimy coating on them so were very slippery. We would get soaked for sure going all the way behind falls, so we didn't. Instead, we crossed just after the pooling of water several yards downriver. We went jumping from rock-to-rock and laughing, especially when one of us slipped and splashed a foot in the water!

This was the most beautiful day to spend here, with

the sun brightly glistening on the water and baking the rocks. We all settled on large smooth boulders. We spread towels out and laid down and soaked up the sun for a bit.

After a while, one of our friends, who suggested this spot, finally told us the reason he brought us here. He explained that the river level and flow was far higher than normal, so you could sit down in the water between the big boulders and the current would sweep you down the river! The current was fast, and when we looked down route, we could see patches of turbulent

Photo credit: daniilphotos on 123rf

white water here and there, meaning possibly rocks underneath.

We were all reluctant to get in, so we encouraged our friend who suggested this location to show us first. Afterall, it was his idea! With his shoes off, he stood up in the refreshingly cold, fast-flowing river. He was a bit unstable at first standing up from the power of the water. We were watching with excitement, and quietly wondering if we were going to be the next to do this or not. He then sat down in the water, and quickly outstretched his legs in front of him. He was immediately whisked off down river to the cheers of excitement and thrill of the rest of us on both sides of him! We watched as he went through the turbulent sections with no yelps of pain from hitting any underwater rocks, so we had seen enough and in we went one-by-one following his lead with great excitement.

The power of the river was immense, and you had to be firmly positioned just to stand in the water flow. The first time I was swept down the river, it was pure excitement, so thrilling. As soon as I sat down in the water, I was whisked away whilst quickly shooting my feet up and out in front of me. I was swept along in a seated position with my feet frequently bobbing up out of the water. I didn't have much choice as to which way I went, as the current was so strong, and the boulders somewhat guided you along until there were no more boulders and the river widened. At that stage, the flow of the river slowed and was less turbulent. At the end of the run, I hopped out of the water and onto a boulder and made my way back up the river and to do it all again. It was amazing, so much fun!

After several times there were only a couple of us still

doing it. The others had taken to their towels and were soaking up the sun again. I had done several runs by now and I'd noticed at the other end of the route there was a fork in the flow. I'd tried a couple of times to go to the right, but the river kept sweeping me along to the left with its immense power. The next time, I was determined to go to the right and nothing was going to stop me! I was going to make it happen and I was eager to see if it would be an additional thrill to tell the others about.

So, on the next run, when I reached the fork again, this time I purposely threw my legs to the right and figured the water would just sweep the rest of me along in the same direction. Well, that didn't happen! Sure enough, my legs went to the right, but my upper body was still pulled to the left and the rest of me was heading at speed for the big boulder in front that divided the two routes. I knew I was destined to collide with the dividing rock. Although it was going to be a significant impact, I figured it would be fun to talk about it afterwards back upriver with the lads.

So, what seemed like harmless adventurous fun was quickly turning into something a little more serious. I still wasn't too worried, though, and I was going with the flow and relaxed since I figured what could happen beyond a few minor cuts at most. Well, then my body rotated, and my head went underwater, and my back impacted the rock first. The rock must have been curve-shaped from the wear of the water over the years.

I was pinned submerged under the water with my back against the boulder and my legs flailing in the turbulence. What struck me immediately was that the power of the water was immense. I was jammed firmly underwater against that boulder, and I couldn't grab onto anything nor do anything to get free.

I didn't panic as I figured I'd be swept away soon enough, but the water pressure was heavy on my chest, and it suddenly dawned on me that this was fast becoming a very serious situation. I fought to get free, but nothing happened. I fought and fought but

Photo credit: balinature on 123rf

nothing. My hope was that any second now I would be swept along the river, but that didn't happen. After struggling desperately for some time, I realized that the more I struggled the noticeably weaker I became. The power of the water was immense and tiring. This struck me as deeply unfair, since how could I get out of this if I was losing energy! Surely, I'm not meant to die here and now, am I? I hadn't taken a breath for some time now and I was quickly burning through the last of my energy. I didn't feel like I had to gasp for breath, but I was very aware I was way beyond the time I would normally be able to hold my breath for. I was very aware this was now a life-or-death situation.

All the struggling hadn't had any effect at all. Eventually, I had pretty much no energy left, and I found myself looking up through the brightly illuminated, bubble-filled, turbulent water and thinking that I would dearly love to be above the water again enjoying the summer sun. I'd love to be sitting on the rocks spending the afternoon just soaking up the sun again and enjoying the majesty of the river running through the picturesque tree-lined gorge. I realized the world up there was so spectacularly beautiful! More beautiful than I'd ever appreciated before all of this had happened. What I would give just to be back up there enjoying the day again without a worry in the world.

Mom's response will come at the end of the next course, as these two courses are strongly linked.

FIRST MAIN COURSE

Mom, I hope you are still holding tightly onto that pillow, because you'll need it for just a little longer! I know this near-death experience is difficult for you to hear but learning about what happened will hopefully be worthwhile. Enjoy.

In that moment, I was looking up through the brightly lit, turbulent, bubbly water. I realized that the chapters of my life, unfolding for almost two decades, were now coming to an abrupt and wholly unexpected end. These are my very last moments alive; literally my life's ending right this second! I'd had my last breath a long time ago and I knew I was taking the last obscured glimpses of sunlight from this beautiful world; a world I now realized I hardly knew and wanted to experience more of. Was this all there was meant for me? No wife, no family of my own, no career, no travel, no more existing—nothing more to this life? In that moment, I realized just how beautiful life was—just to experience it, just to savor it, just to observe it, just to be—and then my thoughts turned to my family finding out that I'd died right now, right here. Who would explain it to them? Incredibly, I could literally feel and see the book of life closing over on my life! Time was ending abruptly for me and, shockingly, the full story of my life was now all written! How could that be? The world and sunlight were about to disappear forever.

At that point, everything momentarily went black and suddenly I was no longer in the river. I couldn't feel the water nor the boulder pressing against me anymore. I couldn't feel any turbulence which was making it so difficult to orientate myself, and all was completely quiet now. I was completely calm, quiet, and collected. I had been literally plucked out of that desperate situation, and I was gently gliding along in a space that was like no other that I'd previously experienced.

It was like the world and time had literally disappeared and didn't matter anymore. All the concerns I had in the river were also gone. It was like I was now in an infinite space. Visually, it was like seeing a beautiful night sky and being in it at the same time. I was moving relative to a surface just below me, and I was looking towards the left of the direction that I was travelling. As I continued forwards, I turned to look more straight-on, as I could see and feel this absorbing all-pervading white light coming from in front of me. The white light wasn't just light, it was like it was felt throughout all of me, all at once. It was somewhat like sunbathing, and perhaps we enjoy sunbathing on earth so much because it reminds us of this light. It felt so good as it bathed me with an eternal warmth, energy, and love. A truly unparalleled experience. If you are a

Photo credit: wangshuangpaul on 123rf

Christian, then you will surely believe this was the Holy Spirit or God.

I kept moving like I was gliding gently forwards towards the light, but I was still looking somewhat to the left. I could sense some spirits and started receiving communication from them now. The messages I was receiving were gentle and loving and were encouraging me home, to turn into the light, and to cross over.

I had the distinct impression that my time on earth had just been a short temporary experience and I felt that going into the light was really like returning home. The best way I can describe it, is it was like I had just recovered from amnesia, and this world beyond was my real long-lost home with numerous spirits who were so familiar and brought me love, warmth, and all manner of family feelings.

As much as I loved my family back on earth, it felt like my eyes were opened to the fact that earth was just a temporary experience and unimportant now. I recall looking more towards the light to see where the other communications were coming from, as I knew that some communications were coming directly from within the light and some from the side.

Just to the left, I saw a group of spirits in what seemed like a network or structure. It was made up of

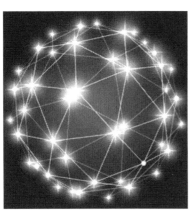

individual spirits, but they appeared to be connected in some way exchanging thoughts and feelings with one another. It was incredible to observe. As well as this group of spirits exchanging communications, individual spirits

Photo credit: Tzido Sun on Shutterstock

within the network were also sending me messages directly. This whole network surprised and overwhelmed me a little and without saying anything the spirits sensed this and reorganized to make it more comfortable for me. Many of the individual spirits separated off from the network to be more easily recognizable. Communication then came from those individual spirits, one-at-a-time. I could see the spirits more easily now and it's like I could see attributes of each of these spirits from their past time on earth.

It's like these individual spirits had a history from living in the world that could be seen, but I should make it clear that their history wasn't the essence of the spirit here. It didn't even seem particularly important at all now. The spirits were pure and independent and had a unique character with or without allowing me to see their past traits. Seeing the individual spirits and glimpsing their histories made it more comfortable and familiar for me though.

The mode of communication with the spirits was unusual. When the spirits were communicating with me, I could see the messages being sent to me in a really unique way. As I received a message, I could see the information unpack and then wash over me and surprisingly also the feelings along with it! It was incredibly unique communication but mimicked what we have on earth at least in some respects, although on earth it is far more limited. It was astonishing to receive more than just words in a message. Sure, I am used to words eliciting emotions but in this case the emotions were wrapped up in the message and washed over me when I received it. It's as though I could directly experience the thoughts and emotions of these individual spirits.

It seemed to me that because of this way of communicating, the spirits here were far more intimately connected than people in the world. When they sent a message, I could see it being packaged up, and then it would come to me, unpack, and wash over me with information and emotions. I could also see it on-route as well, it was incredible! The individual spirits that were communicating with me were so familiar, yet I didn't recognize any of them as specific people that I'd previously known on earth; however, I suppose at the time I hadn't known many people who had died. What was evident was their spirit essence. It felt like they were my family, my relatives you would say. In fact, I felt like I'd known them for much longer than my earthly family.

Just to the right of those spirits, I was communicating with a spirit who was fully in the light and was also encouraging me to cross over. I don't think the spirit was a judge of my actions on earth, but rather was just determining if I had had the requisite experience in the world to be able to cross over. It felt like it was a far more important spirit and had an important role. It is possible it was God or the spirit of Jesus or perhaps just a gate-keeper spirit, I don't know for sure. Anything is possible but I knew if I turned fully toward that spirit in the light then I would have crossed over for sure.

There was also an immense feeling of love, and it was incredibly appealing just to look into the light and cross over. It looked so lovely existing and interacting there as a spirit. As mentioned, the group of spirits that I first saw were in a big structure of interacting spirits. This must be what it is like to be completely close with others, even explicitly a part of others' thoughts and emotions. Perhaps even existing as a shared experience! This must be far beyond experiencing things together with others on earth, beyond what is possible with marriage or friendship. It was as if the spirits were at times fully interconnected with one another here. So, think of a brain with all the connected neurons, but instead of neurons replace them with independent spirits.

So, the network of individual spirits could experience as a whole and could be directly a part of what other spirits experienced. Of course, when desired, the spirits could separate into individual spirits as well with their own character, history, and autonomy. The spirits were beautifully pure in form and in that networked structure it looked harmonious and wonderful and must be incredible to experience.

The spirits were so overjoyed that I was there and warmly welcomed and encouraged me to cross, but I recall hesitating to turn into the light. It was so appealing on so many levels, so what was stopping me? I recall a partial wall appearing on the left side of my view with the infinite space around it. A globe of the earth then appeared on the wall. When I looked at the globe, it enabled me to recall being in the world and with the people and experiences of life there. It was partly visual, but it was like I could experience the feelings of people in the world as well. I got a clear sense of what it was like to be back on earth. I had a sense of home and my family, friends and life more generally. I could, from a distance, experience life back on earth again, for the moment at least. I clearly realized that I didn't long to be back there, even though it was a loving place.

Upon seeing people moving about in their lives doing this and that, it then struck me very clearly, in an epiphany, that what people in the world mostly think about, focus on, and worry about isn't important in the grand scheme of things. It struck me very deeply that, here, none of it mattered very much at all. It felt strange that people in the world didn't really clearly know there was life after death. It was crystal clear to me that all these earthly things people were concentrating on were not the reason for being in the world. They may feel all important to us when in the world, but they are not important in the bigger picture. Moreover, none of the things being focused on were particularly important in terms of crossing over at death, either.

It was incredible to think that people back on earth were not aware there was this world beyond that they would return to after dying. In fact, it was from here that we all originated from. These were epiphanies, but they didn't come with full realization at the time of what our purpose on earth was. It struck me that I was privy to these important insights, and I wanted to share them with people back on earth. The spirit-in-the-light asked, 'if I was ready [to cross over] now' and, surprisingly, I said 'no'.

Now don't get me wrong, crossing over was attractive on all levels, in every regard. You cannot believe how compelling it was, but I still replied 'no'. It just felt right. The spirit asked me 'why, what is preventing you [from crossing]?' I took a moment of spirit awareness, glanced back at the earth, and what came to me was 'I have more to do [in the world]'.

It was a vague answer to be perfectly honest and it took me considerable time to understand it myself. To be fair, I was ready to cross over. There wasn't anything back in the world more appealing. But I had these two impressions when I made the decision not to cross. One was that people didn't really know that this world beyond death existed! The other was that people were focusing on all manner of things in this world but most of it wasn't relevant to the experience we needed to gain from this world and to prepare for crossing over at death. It didn't seem fair that I would just leave now and take this understanding with me.

To be fair, I wasn't sure I would be allowed to return with this new understanding, though. At the time, I felt I could share the message if I returned to earth, and it would help people. People on earth were wrapped up in all manner of things in life yet very little of it had any relevance in terms of why we had this earthly experience in the first place. I understood that what was more important in terms of crossing over was whether you were ripe to cross. And, whether you were ripe was not directly related to what people on earth were spending so much time and energy on. It was clear that the spirit-in-the-light had expected I would cross and would have preferred that I did.

The spirits I saw were so loving, warm, and encouraging that it was so incredibly difficult not to cross, but I felt I would be okay returning to the world, especially with the knowledge of what was beyond. The spirit-in-the-light then asked me 'what more do you have to do?' I replied with certainty, 'I don't know, but I have more to do'. I felt completely congruent with this response.

The spirit-in-the-light, along with at least one other spirit forensically analyzed me top-to-bottom like a literal scan for something, perhaps truth. I suppose that if they felt I was fearful to cross, then they would probably have encouraged me even more, or something else. Once they had finished analyzing me, I felt a momentary pause and then I recall hearing a faint communication from another assisting spirit reporting to the spirit-in-the-light. The spirit quietly reported with some concern questioning whether my physical body back in the river was still usable. That was the last comment I heard beyond.

A moment later, I was back in the river struggling for my life again. The current was just so strong, and I could feel the pressure of the water and turbulence pressing on me again. Externally, that quiet peacefulness was gone. It was certainly clear that I was

Photo credit: balinature on 123rf

still trapped. I don't recall my eyes being open at all now. I tried to struggle, but I recall clearly thinking to myself that I am still going to die and go beyond again! What's the reason for returning here if I'm going straight back there again? I didn't have any fear at all, but it just didn't seem to make sense to me. It was like the universe was out of its natural order again.

In that moment, I received a communication that came to me as a thought, but in a subtly different way to my normal worldly thoughts. I was still in a pure state of spirit awareness, so I observed this individual thought as it arose, as well as the way it arose. It came to me in a very similar way to what I experienced beyond, but it was like there was a barrier now between this world and the spirit world, at least a semi-permeable

53

barrier. The message came through in an unusual way. It is like I could perceive it initiate and then it was like it bubbled up through the barrier which now separated our world from the spirit world. The message instructed me to reach with my hand in a certain way and incrementally grasp at what little traction was there. To move myself little-by-little with one hand in an awkward and seemingly ineffective way.

I had no idea at this stage which way was up or down. Once I had done this hand movement for a little while, I received another communication that again bubbled up through the semi-permeable barrier and unpacked into my awareness. It now said to push in a certain way. I had evidently managed to turn myself part-way around and was being instructed to push against the boulder or ground; I wasn't exactly sure which way was up at this point. I was sure I was now pushing my body against the current and so I held it like that for a moment or two.

Suddenly, I was swept away from being pinned against the boulder, and I resurfaced. I emerged back into the air and back into the sunlight of this beautiful world! I had survived and was alive! I desperately gasped for breath and saw a friend standing on the boulder in front of me. I crawled onto that boulder with encouragement and help from him. As I struggled to get out of the water, I knew I was at the limit of exhaustion. At the same time, I was truly shocked to see everyone all over the boulders at this end of the route all looking for me downriver. When I went under the water, they were all lying around at the top-end of the route sunbathing and taking no notice. My friend must have alerted them.

I sought to stand up as quickly as I could, but it was difficult. I had some unusual difficulty breathing. I pressed on and got moving though. I stood up on the boulder as others were chatting and heading back upriver to their patches in the sun, now that all the commotion was over.

My friend asked me quietly and very intently, 'where were you?' He continued, 'you were gone a *long* time.' 'Everyone thought you were certainly swept downriver by now and had drowned for sure'. I asked him how long I was gone for because he looked so astonished. He paused for a moment and tried to estimate, and he replied that he didn't know but said emphatically 'it was *long*'. I realized it must have been long to have mobilized the guys and get them all searching. That would have taken some time since my friends wouldn't have noticed I was gone right away, and he wouldn't have mobilized everyone until he was sure that something had really gone wrong.

He then came in close and really pressed me for where I went. It was like he was saying 'just tell me and you don't have to share what happened with the others. This shocked me, as it felt like he really knew where I'd gone. I closed-up and shrugged him off, as I was still processing it. I just kind of ignored him and his questions as much as possible and started walking slowly and changed the subject. I gave him the impression that nothing happened, but I knew something very significant had. I closed-up and suppressed the experience. In fact, I really suppressed it as I didn't mention it to anyone except my wife for most of my life. I told my kids once they were old enough to understand and I told only a couple of close friends in recent years.

What could I have done when I came out of the water, tell everyone that nothing matters! That what everyone is focusing on in life is relatively unimportant! I had an incredible experience and some important insights but what could I do with them? I was a teenager and more interested in socializing and having fun than writing books. Besides, the internet and mobile phones didn't even exist yet! At the time, you pretty much could only tell things to the people near you, and that was it. I also didn't have a clear message that was ready to be received by anyone. The near-death experience had just been imposed on me, essentially against my will. I certainly needed time to understand it myself. I felt powerless and unprepared to spread any message now that I was back in the world.

The idea of telling everyone somehow felt far more challenging now that I was back immersed in the world again. It certainly planted a seed in me, though, to understand as much as I could about this world. I didn't make the connection at the time, but I had this innate curiosity about what we knew of the world. This curiosity really blossomed and became more focused as well. Because of this experience, I delved a little into metaphysics to find out what people thought about this world and what was said about after death, but quickly realized nothing was satisfying. Furthermore, there weren't many ways to find out information back then. I also sought to understand about religion, including what was specifically said by the prophets like Jesus and other spiritual leaders like Buddha.

I decided I also wanted to know what science said about this world. The scientific approach seemed to be more concrete at describing the world, certainly of what could be measured and understood. So, I pursued becoming a scientist by studying physical science to learn as much as possible about the inner workings of the physical world.

All of this came many years after the river experience. The connection to my near-death experience wasn't obvious at the time, but I see it clearly now upon reflecting on everything. All this learning about the world was a lengthy process and occurred over the course of my life so far. Some of it turned into my career and other parts became my interests and hobbies. I kept my near-death experience locked-up tightly. I knew it was an important experience that I wasn't fully able to understand until recently, though.

So, why write this book now? Well, mom, with your health issues in recent years and with Covid-19 causing deaths disproportionately to your generation, I felt some urgency to write this book to help you to understand from my experiences what is beyond death. I felt it would be important to describe to you about this experience of dying (and other related experiences) so that it would bring you comfort and assurance that there is life after death. I also wanted to write this book so there was an accurate record of my experiences and thoughts for my kids and others to read. I have told my kids about my experiences, but I also wanted to write it down for them so they could reread it later in life, perhaps when I am long-gone, and they are thinking of such things.

I should have done this a long time ago. Ideally before dad passed, but life's responsibilities were too demanding at the time. It is also important that I wrote this book for others to read. This links back to my original purpose for returning to this world, so I am honored if others are reading this now. My hope is not to tell you the way things are and for you to just believe it. Rather, it is to let you know what happened to me and what I think about the 'world beyond' based on my experiences. If this strikes a chord as consistent with what you feel, then wonderful; perhaps it is just putting words and experiences to what you intuitively know.

Preamble to mom's response

Mom, I know it was difficult to hear all of this. I realise no parent wants to hear about their child struggling for their life! Consequently, I didn't tell you about this experience until now. Mom, your comments from our discussion are below.

Mom's response to the First Main Course

I'm certainly glad you told me of this experience. It has taken a while to absorb and digest it all. I was mesmerized by this course. I felt that it was really sad that you were under the water wishing you were back up above! On one hand, it must have been incredibly hard for you and on the other hand it turned out to be a wonderful experience. I had to take a deep breath when you were reading this to me. How would someone handle being asked to turn into the light! I suppose it just wasn't the right time and you wanted to come back. That is wonderful how you described the emotions from the spirits unpacking and washing over you, it sounds wonderful.

You mentioned that people aren't focusing on what they should on earth, but people must handle the things of daily life. What can you do besides be kind, pray, and care for people? Isn't that interesting how it struck you about people and wanting to return to tell them. I think that was your duty and I'm glad you are fulfilling it. It's helpful to let people know these things. I know that after hearing about this experience the fear of dying has drained away. It sounds beautiful beyond, and I now view death like an adventure. I'm certainly grateful for you sharing your experiences with me!

PALATE CLEANSER COURSE

Mom, we are now entering the part of the book where I discuss the meaning contained in my experiences. But first, let's cleanse the palate with thinking about one of life's most important questions. If you take away, as I did, from my near-death experience that the world beyond is a beautiful, compassionate, and loving place, then a fundamental question arises. It's a question that seems also to be at the heart of why young people have turned away from believing in God. Mom, enjoy this course. It will certainly cleanse your palate!

Before we proceed, I'd like to mention that I refer to God numerous times in the next few courses. Mom, you believe in God and that is why I have written it in this way. However, I just wanted to make it very clear for those other readers who may not

61

believe in God that it is perfectly fine to consider what is presented in the context of just a spirit world existing beyond.

Mom, brace yourself! If you want something to potentially shake your religious and even spiritual foundations to the core, then consider the following question. Why do innocent young children die every day of illnesses such as leukemia? Put another way, and more generally, some people go through horrendously difficult lives, yet others have a relatively easy time in life. It doesn't seem to be related to how good a person you are.

The question is fundamental to answer for a person questioning the existence of God or spirituality in general. Why would such injustices occur if there is a fair and loving God in existence? I am sure this question not only unsettles religious people, but it also provides significant justification for the younger generation to disbelieve religion and spirituality.

So how can such horrific injustices be rationalized with a God that is reported to be all-powerful, all-knowing, and all-good? Over the centuries, people have developed many ways to address this question. Some people believe God favors them and not others. That may make sense up until bad things happen to the favored people. Or they may believe God is angry with them or is testing their faith. In the modern era, these aren't satisfactory answers and are inconsistent with my near-death experience of a fair and loving God and spirit world. Others think they are special and living charmed lives for some reason, or God has a special purpose for them, so they are somehow exempt from the injustices.

I recall my dad expressing that he believed in God; he felt something was there. He served in the second world war and I'm sure he felt he survived, in part, due to someone above looking out for him. I don't doubt that he had a sense of something being there; however, I was left wondered about all the others serving with him who did die. Let's even consider the extreme, for example, a priest doing God's work getting struck down in a deadly car accident. Can we justify that? Was the priest needed in heaven?

Others rationalize the injustices by appealing to karma. I certainly believe in the earthly form of karma, such that, if you are a murderer and you end up being murdered then it wasn't a surprise. However, if reincarnation does exist then perhaps karma across different lives is possible, but I'm extremely doubtful that there would be horrific injustices for so many as consequence. So, karma doesn't seem to be the answer, either. There was no tallying up of good and bad deeds that I was aware of when I was invited to cross over.

Large numbers of religious people conclude that God just works in mysterious ways. The theory is that His actions are beyond our comprehension as humans. So, there are reasons why bad things happen to good people, and vice versa, but humans just cannot understand the reasoning behind it. Thus, either we don't know enough, or God is working with some sort of other logic. I would find it very difficult to believe that basic reasoning wouldn't make sense if you could know all the information, as we expect God does. So, let's retain logic. But we may not know enough to understand what is going on and that may be the case, but where is the explanation? The justifications seem to be endless and complicated.

I do believe we can make sense out of the injustices that occur in this world. It will take some effort so I will present what I believe over the next few courses. Most certainly, I will base the explanation as much as possible on my near-death experience. I believe we should tackle this question of why horrific injustices occur with the following in mind. First, requiring any explanation to be consistent with what happened during my near-death experience; second, we should question what is assumed about God; and third, really question why God would want a world such as ours and the people in it. There are some incredible things contained in the near-death experience so we will discuss each of them over the next courses before coming to any conclusion.

We can, however, start to lay the groundwork now. Let us take stock of what we know and then look at assumptions about God in light of my near-death experience. To start with, we must accept that horrific injustices are a fact of life, and our world provides an abundance of that sort of proof. I'm sure you don't doubt this claim but let's stop seeking to explain it away and instead just accept it as evidence. Next, I conclude from my near-death experience that the spirit world exists, and God likely exists as well. Now, most of this book does not hinge upon you believing in God, but there is nothing more to say if you don't believe anything exists beyond this world. So, we will move forward with at least a spirit world existing.

As mentioned previously, if you are uncomfortable with accepting the existence of God then think about 'spirit world' when I refer to God in the following. As an aside, I refer to God as male but don't take it literally and think of him like a person. Next, I would advocate that God (or the spirit world, if you prefer) is fair and loving, based on my near-death experience. Lastly, assuming God exists (or the spiritual world) then He should be acting to save people from experiencing horrific injustices.

I suspect people turn away from believing in God since He (or the spiritual world) doesn't have an obvious presence in the world and isn't seen to be saving people. Thus, for many people, God appears to be absent. For those afflicted by cruel diseases or in horrendous circumstances, this must seem particularly saddening. So, we have a difficult task ahead of us. I struggled with all of this for many years but believe there is a rational explanation based on the evidence from my near-death experience. I will explain.

So now we will question assumptions about God. Implicit in many peoples' beliefs about God are that He is all-knowing, all-powerful, and all-good. From my near-death experience, I would propose that God has had to suspend one or more of these powers in our world. It may be for good reason, though. For instance, God may have had to temporarily limit all-powerfulness so may not be able to act fully in this world for some reason. I will give you a very simple analogy that will hopefully make this a little clearer.

Let's say you own a bicycle, and you are very mechanically minded. You have dismantled the bike into its individual components many times and rebuilt it each time, perfectly. You might say that you are all-powerful with regards to dismantling, reassembling, and fixing your bike. Now, you set off on your journey riding the bike somewhere. All is going well until you incur a puncture in one of your tires. Now, you are all-powerful in terms of being able to repair your bike, and you can easily repair a simple puncture. However, you couldn't fully exercise that ability whilst you are still riding the bike. Obviously, but the point is that even someone with all-powerfulness may have to suspend or limit certain powers to achieve some aim of doing something or getting somewhere. Later, I will make a similar justification as to why God wouldn't interact in this world while it is evolving, even to stop injustices.

So, we have taken a few steps towards addressing why there are horrific injustices in this world that has a fair and loving God or spirit world in existence. So far, I have suggested that God may need to suspend all-powerfulness in this world and consequently may not be able to stop these injustices. I haven't explained why yet, but for now we can recognize there are consequences to suspending powers in this world. If God is not tracking nor controlling how this world evolves then it is free to evolve however it will and that can, unavoidably, lead to both good and bad outcomes.

There is another consequence of suspending all-powerfulness which is really very beneficial for us. I will outline it all soon enough, along with the journey that I believe God has us on. But first, I need to outline what I've learned from my near-death experience which will be presented over the next two courses.

Preamble to mom's response

Mom, the answer to this challenging question of 'why do children die of leukemia if there is a caring a loving God' will become clear as I tell you more in the coming courses about what I take from the near-death experience. The question isn't easy to answer but is really important since it is key to understanding this world we live in and has far-reaching consequences. In the extreme, I expect that people have even concluded the existence of hell because of misinterpreting God's actions in this world. I will come back to answer this Palate Cleanser question fully in a later course, after I have first described a few more points from my near-death experience. Mom, your comments are as follows.

Mom's response to the Palate Cleanser Course

Why children die from leukemia seems to be a question that no one can answer, and it is terribly sad that it happens at all. I agree, many of the ways that people try to explain it are dissatisfying. We were brought up to believe that we were being looked out for, but over time things don't always work out for everyone. You say that you can explain it, so I look forward to that over the next few courses.

The last few ideas were very challenging to absorb. They will take some time to digest, but I certainly agree that God may not be able to do everything all the time. When we discussed this material, it became clearer that you are saying God may need to suspend powers to allow us to go on a journey in this world but there are consequences of allowing that.

SECOND MAIN COURSE

Mom, in the first main course, I told you what happened to me moment-by-moment during my near-death experience. In this course, I will tell you what I derive from that experience. Once you digest this course, and a few other reflections in the next course, I will then return to that key life question posed in the last course about why there are horrific injustices in this world if there is a fair and loving God. Enjoy!

Many interesting points come to mind from my near-death experience. Certainly, the overarching take-away for me is that you don't disappear into nothingness when you physically die. This is momentous for those who experience a near-death event. Consequently, if I took nothing else from the experience then that would certainly be enough.

Doubters of this whole experience might believe I was just searching for something to exist after life; however, as outlined in my childhood experience, I wasn't expecting anything to come after death. My near-death experience has changed all that for me now, though. It is wonderful to know that there is a spirit within us—that observer—that will continue after death.

When you know there is life after death then it seems, at first, paradoxical that you don't take forward the mind/body since that is what people identify with and cultivate throughout their life. The body that you look at in the mirror each day and sense the world through. Your mind, with all those familiar ways of thinking including wants, desires, idiosyncrasies, strengths, and faults, which all appear to make up 'you'.

So, you may be wondering, do you lose the 'you' when you die? What is left? Well, what is left is hard to describe, but it is the core of you that seamlessly goes onwards after death. It is the pure awareness that you experience the world through; it is 'you the perceiver' behind all those thoughts and feelings that distort our awareness. It is the fundamental observer within you that perceives quietly all the time.

To experience the spirit awareness, just be aware of what is behind the thoughts and feelings that come and go. Those thoughts and feelings are just manifestations of the physical world, obscurations to experiencing your spirit awareness. As I sit here writing this and looking across a beautiful Yorkshire valley, the mind/body naturally quietens in the presence of nature, and if you don't have much on your mind then you're able to experience moments of the spirit awareness within. This is why people like to spend time in nature and feel centered by it.

Let me make a distinction here, what I experienced during my near-death experience was my pure spirit existing completely independent of my mind/body. My spirit was no longer in my body, and I was existing purely in the spirit form. Whereas, what we typically experience in this world is a more limited spirit awareness. This is what we experience as we normally view the world through the window of the mind/body.

To recognize your spirit awareness as distinct from the mind/body then you should do meditation, walks in nature, prayer, spiritual practice, etc. The spirit awareness is innate in all of us and accessible to all, everyone in society. Once you get a felt sense of your spirit awareness within, then you can experience it even in the presence of mind/body obscurations. So, mom, we don't disappear into nothingness at death. The mind/body strips away and your spirit goes forward and will fully manifest in the spirit world beyond.

After having this near-death experience and knowing the spirit continues, it has changed my perspective on life. I realized that the focus in this world should be on the spirit, not the mind/body. Once you realise there is part of you that continues after death, then the other parts become less important in terms of your purpose here in the world. I realized that by focusing on the spirit within, then it becomes clear that the mind/body is only the vehicle for the spirit to experience this world through. An important vehicle, but a vehicle none-the-less.

Human history has a long track-record of having the wrong focus, and I believe our current focus on the mind/body, in essence, the physical aspects of living are more examples of this incorrect focus. This incorrect focus has happened many times in human history and in very significant ways in the past. Take, for example, when people used to believe that all the planets revolved around the earth, and we were the central focus of the universe. It made sense at the time, but with hindsight, humans just got caught up with putting themselves at the center.

Similarly, it appears to make logical sense that people would naturally put the focus of their life on the physical mind/body. The focus ends up on all things mind and body, though. What you need, and all manner of what you want. This is especially the case in a materialistic society. However, the change in perspective that came from my near-death experience made me realise this is incorrect. Our focus is mostly off and has been for a long time. Perhaps some traditional communities in some ways strike a better balance, but those ways are not yet properly integrated with modern society.

During my near-death experience, when I was

moving along towards the light, it was apparent that I had no body, I was just in pure spirit form. I wasn't walking in the spirit world, I was gliding smoothly along, and I didn't feel any physical sensations. It didn't really matter to me that I was without a body since I felt complete, and I didn't feel any need to cling to the physical form that was dying in the water. This is important to note, that you shouldn't cling. You would only cling to the mind/body if you are not ready to relinquish the world and reside exclusively in the spirit form. If that is the case, then you are saying yourself that you need more time in the world, perhaps another life experience.

Just to give you a little more insight about the world beyond, I'll tell you a little more about what it was like to exist wholly in the spirit form. My awareness was pure with no mind thoughts and no obscurations cluttering-up perception. I was in a pure single-pointed spirit awareness with perfect clarity. There were no competing thoughts or ideas, no plans being made, no history revisited. It was just a single flow of awareness and existing. It was a beautiful and pure state.

Now some people might panic from not having a body but think about it for a minute. Your mind/body have been changing substantially over your whole lifetime. Your mind/body are nothing like what they were when you were a teenager, let alone at birth. Literally nothing like it! You might be able to tell that one evolved from the other, but nothing is the same,

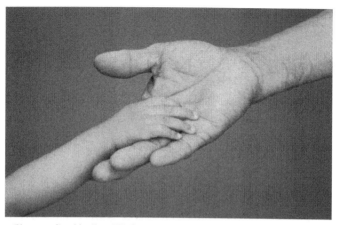

Photo credit: phloxii on 123rf

literally nothing. So, yes, it is sad to think about losing your mind/body, but you have lost it over and over throughout your life. It has just been a slow and continuous process of change, so it hasn't alarmed you. I want to share with you an analogy that I think is a nice way to think of the mind/body/spirit and death.

Imagine you have a valuable brooch with a beautiful diamond in the center and an intricate metal design surrounding that diamond. This brooch is special to you, and you have grown very attached to the design, and it is the only one you wear. However, the brooch has now aged and parts of it have become broken. What do you do now that it is no longer usable? Well, undoubtably you experience sadness at the loss of the beautiful design, but then you extract the diamond (if you recognize its value) and use it in another surround or admire it on its own. You don't endlessly mourn the broken surround, nor throw away the diamond when you discard the rest of the brooch. Yes, you lost something special to you, but that diamond will continue onwards and will remain unchanged and unaffected.

In a similar way to the brooch surround, your mind/body is temporary and wears out, and one day will need discarding. But importantly, you have a diamond within you that is your spirit that continues after death and should be the focus of why you are in this world. Even if you don't have a near-death experience, the world gives you indications that this is the right way to view things, since your mind/body are continuously changing and aging.

In fact, the whole lifecycle seems to be key. Thinking back to when you were a baby, you might have welcomed change since you grew larger, stronger, more capable, and independent. But, the change has been non-stop throughout your life, sometimes for the better and sometimes for the worse. So, if you view the spirit as the focus of your life, then you will see that the deterioration of the mind/body highlights their insignificance, rather than the aging process acting to trigger you to cling and fear death.

From my near-death experience, being unattached to the mind/body and world, in general, felt to be a necessary requirement for crossing-over. I suspect those who cling to the world will return to it again. Anyway, life usually gives you decades to come to this realization about the spirit within and to relinquish attachment to the mind/body. As an interesting aside, perhaps people labelled as 'old souls' are either those who are unfortunately too attached to this world, enjoyed life too much and keep returning, or they were taken young in a previous life and have now returned.

So, during my near-death experience it was clear that people in the world largely have the wrong focus. They put huge effort into what isn't important in the longer run for the spirit world. After experiencing my spirit within and knowing it continues beyond and the mind and body don't, then the logical focus must instead be the spirit. This is not to say that your mind/body aren't important—they are, but it is about where you place your focus that is important.

With the focus on the spirit, it follows that the world is likely some sort of 'experience ground' for the spirit within you. I would go as far as to say a nursery for the spirit. The spirit within you experiences the world *through* the mind/body. The spirit experiences the *full* human lifecycle (and this world as well) and then returns to the spirit world. The spirit must obviously need to gain something from this experience.

What could it need to gain? Well, if you look at the lifecycle of the mind/body, then it offers a plausible explanation. Humans are born, learn to function in this world, grow and mature in which they develop an identity, become independent, take on responsibility, and then finally age and die. The spirit doesn't latch onto the body mid-way through life, nor does it leave before death—it is here for the whole lifecycle. So, the full lifecycle must be important for the spirit as well.

Let's look at this a little closer. As the baby is developing over time into a toddler, it realizes its independence, and its character and identity develop. In parallel, perhaps the spirit is doing something similar. I believe that the spirit, through its experience within the human body, comes to know its own independent nature and character.

In this first step of paralleling the human growth, what happens is that the spirit naturally comes to see itself as *being* the mind/body. It benefits from this development and growth, but at the same time unfortunately *identifies* with the mind/body. So, it develops independence, but it isn't independent of the mind/body for the time being.

The second fundamental step in life is when the spirit gains its own autonomy or independence from the mind/body. Everyone must realise this for themselves, within their own lifetime. So, the spirit within you must learn to distinguish between what is mind/body and what is spirit. The natural aging process of the mind/body steps in to help us with this. The peeling away of the mind/body with age is the process that aims to achieve this; however, many people unfortunately don't recognize that the spirit is even within them at all, and so they believe there is nothing left as the body ages, faulters, and dies. It is a sad circumstance indeed.

If we return to the brooch example, the person is so attached to the design of the brooch, that the beautiful diamond in the core is frequently overlooked since perhaps it has long been covered over with the grit and dirt of life. In the end, the person focuses on the loss of the brooch as a whole. That endearing shape and design, and thinks the brooch is completely worn out and ready to be completely discarded. They haven't seen or thought about the diamond core since they were a child and have forgotten all about it.

My hope is for you to recognize that diamond within, and to know that you, like the diamond, will continue beyond. Mom, the way you recognize that diamond is to be aware of that within you which doesn't appear to age with time. It just isn't of the physical realm.

Unfortunately, our modern society doesn't understand that we should respect these latter years of life as crucially important for the spirit, nor do most older people. The elderly person will have already developed an identity and independence. If the elderly person now realizes their spirit within and identifies with it, then they have completed the key purpose of being in this world. That is, to enable their spirit to gain awareness of its identity, grow through association with the life experience, and to eventually know it's independent of the mind/body. With all this complete, now the person will be ready to cross over.

It is so important that we value the elderly people and help and support them to realise their spirit within.

Certainly, the spiritual wisdom of a society should be measured by how the society perceives and treats their elderly generation, and indeed how the elderly generation perceives themselves and their role in later life.

In summary, there is a spirit attached to the mind/body and it undergoes the development mentioned above of growth, maturing, and then eventually faltering and deterioration of the body, leaving only the spirit to return to the realm beyond. The whole life process suggests to me that our spirits are in this world to undergo development from their experience of being linked to, and seeing the world through, the mind/body.

The mind/body is a temporary vehicle to facilitate self-recognition and development of an independent spirit identity within. So, rather than us focusing only on our mind/body, we should instead focus on recognising and cultivating the spirit within. Additionally, we should be seeking to recognize the spirit within others in preparation for the spirit world beyond. Too often, we only focus on the mind/body and miss the big picture, especially in this modern scientific-based world.

So, mom, I hope you will recognize that you are comprised of a spirit and a mind/body with the latter peeling away. I hope you are comfortable with this. Best to think of it as an incredible new adventure in which that inner core diamond within you goes on. I know how optimistic you are and how much you like adventures. Well, this is the greatest adventure of your life!

Preamble to mom's response

Mom, this has outlined the core way I now view our life in this world based on my near-death experience. When beyond, the epiphany I had was that we were all largely missing the real main focus of our lives in this world. Sure, there are many important things that we must do in life to survive and provide for those around us. But the main focus should be on recognising and developing the spirit within and coming to realise that it is independent of the mind/body. This is largely missed by most. It became clear over time for me that the human lifecycle was the perfect vehicle to bring about this development of the spirit. Mom, your comments from our discussion are below.

Mom's response to the Second Main Course

That is the key message, that you go on after the body dies. This has brought me a lot of peace to hear this. I, too, find walks in nature down by the lake soothes me and are spiritual. That's very interesting what you wrote about the spirit latching onto the baby, developing, and then peeling away. Where did you get all this? It's very intricate. I certainly identify right now with what you say about as you get older. The aging process prepares you for death. The body can't do as much over time and so you need to keep altering what you can do, and you must try new things. Yes, the aging process naturally prepares you to shed the body.

I'm comfortable with my body peeling away and am not afraid of dying now, especially after reading this. I really loved the analogy of the brooch and the diamond and thought it was beautiful about the diamond being the spirit within. I enjoyed the discussion we had about how to cultivate the spirit within and I think all people should understand this. I can recognize this part of me that doesn't age but it is challenging to reside there for long, as thoughts take me off in different directions.

CHEESE COURSE

Mom, here is a selection of other reflections that I thought would be of interest to you that are based on my near-death experience. I hope you enjoy them.

Mom, you may be wondering if I can give my thoughts on what we do in the spirit world after death. I cannot give a complete picture based on my near-death experience because I didn't cross into the light and leave this world completely behind; however, I can give you an impression based on what I did observe. Keep in mind it was a relatively short experience, so I probably saw very little of what spirits do beyond, but here goes.

When I initially observed the spirits, they were connected in that group or network of individual spirits. It was kind of like it was one entity but there were clearly many individual spirits comprising the structure. Numerous individual spirits communicated with me sending me warm, welcoming, reassuring messages of

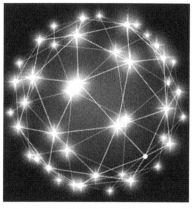

Photo credit: Tzido Sun on Shutterstock

encouragement to cross over. When they communicated, it was like I could get a glimpse into the nature of each individual spirit. All about their character and who they were in the past when they were in the world. It felt like all those spirits who communicated with me were very familiar with me, like I'd known them in the past and they knew me very well.

It looked like the spirits had purpose to their existence. They certainly appeared active, engaged, happy, and fulfilled. It was a beautiful existence with no aging, no illness, and seemingly no hardship. It really was so appealing to cross over and join them. They welcomed me like family and gave me the distinct impression that I was one of many missing pieces of the whole, and they were overjoyed for my return.

Interestingly, when I first saw all the spirits grouped together, it was like they were all connected like the different neurons in a brain. The parallel with a brain is appropriate, as the networked structure of individual spirits gave me the impression they could function as a whole. Perhaps some sort of collective thinking or processing like a brain, even! In any event, they were enjoying the experience together immensely. To join in and be a part of that one day would be incredible to experience.

Mom, as mentioned in the last course, I believe the role of our mind/body on earth is to nurture and be the vehicle for the development of the spirit within us in preparation for this world beyond. This intuitively fits with what I briefly observed. So, you may be wondering if there is something you must do to prepare to cross over into this beautiful world. For example, is it essential to first gain some sort of enlightenment in this lifetime in preparation?

A lot is made of this in the far eastern religions, about escaping the cycle of death and rebirth. Based on my experience, though, I don't believe it is necessary to attain enlightenment to cross over. If you have attained enlightenment, then you will be more prepared than needed, in my opinion. I would say that I was ready to put down my attachment to the world at death, and that was the key, I believe. If you are unemotionally ready to put down your mind/body and go forward wholly as the spirit within, then that is all that is needed. You have gained your independence and identity from this worldly experience and crucially you recognize that at your true core you are spirit.

To return to the brooch and diamond analogy, I

would say that from my experience you must be aware of that diamond within, that spirit awareness. Afterall, it is what continues after death. It therefore helps to be able to see past the obscurations to the spirit awareness prior to passing. Once you recognize the diamond within and are willing to put down the mind/body at death then you are free to appreciate the whole brooch in this world and enjoy its beauty and utility. Just understand that you must not be too attached. Be ready to leave it and not cling to it when the time comes. If you are still clinging to the mind/body at death, then you haven't yet recognized what you need to from your experience in this world.

If you are clinging to your mind/body or the world in any way, and that includes being desperate to leave the world, then you are too attached and its role with you isn't complete. You will need more time with the mind/body/world so you can fully learn to peel away, recognising that the essence of you is the spirit within. So, mom, recognising the spirit awareness within and being prepared so that you relinquish the mind/body/world when the time comes is the essential preparation for crossing over.

As an aside, it seems that many Buddhists and others are exclusively seeking to escape the birth-death cycle, but until your spirit has gained what it needs to from this world then it is valuable to remain in the cycle of reincarnation, if you believe in that. Once you recognize your spirit within and no longer care about leaving the cycle then you are probably ready to cross over.

You may wonder if I have any doubts about my near-death experience. People who doubt near-death experiences usually say that the experience beyond this world was just generated by the mind in response to the near-death event. As a scientist, I must question everything and keep an open mind. There is obviously no proof that I could bring back from the experience to show you, so I can only tell you what I experienced and learned. But I have not read anything convincing that would sway me away from wholeheartedly believing in what I experienced to be true. Of course, I cannot rule anything out, but every inch of me believes it was real.

As I was drowning, I expect I underwent a laryngospasm in which the vocal cords spasmed to close the airway to the lungs. This response would have prevented water from filling my lungs, but it also would have prevented fresh oxygen from entering as well, which is why it is termed dry drowning. It leads to unconsciousness within a couple of minutes and death in several minutes. So, oxygen conservation is crucial. Personally, I think there must be more effective ways for my body to minimize energy usage (and hence oxygen demand) and encourage survival, rather than the brain generating a near-death experience simulation and paradoxically accepting death as incredibly appealing! I can't see that developing from an evolutionary perspective.

The brain runs a 'just in time' delivery of oxygen to the brain's nerve cells and the demands are high when continuously firing, so a simulation of afterlife seems counter to survival when every single oxygen molecule would be valuable and conserved.

You may also be wondering if I still fear death. Yes, I imagine I still do as it is natural to fear huge change, especially with something so drastic as permanently losing the mind/body. Perhaps there is also a residue of fear in the subconscious surrounding death from my childhood. However, I know deep within that what is important is how you move forward at the time of death.

I trust that I will lay down the mind/body/world again at death and will move forward when the time comes. The near-death experience has fundamentally changed my viewpoint about death from one of fear to one of almost certainty about what happens at death and afterwards. Still, I would not be eager to pass at present, as there is still more for me to do in this life, and many obligations to fulfil.

In any event, I have a clear understanding of what will happen to me after death with only minor apprehensions about death itself. In general, I find that many people tend to fear death or block it out completely and ignore it. Most people also have underlying sadness and fear associated with it. This is unfortunate, since it was a beautiful, awe-inspiring experience for me.

Based on my near-death experience, I would explain dying and entering the spirit realm best with another analogy. Pretend for a moment that you live and work in a city. To begin with, you are in the most wonderfully warm and loving home with all your family around you. You are then tasked to go alone on a trip to the city center to get something. So, you walk out the front door into what is a very cold and inhospitable street with icy cold polar winds and rain.

Photo credit: Bist on Shutterstock

After reaching the city center, you trip and fall, hitting your head and you are knocked out for a while. You suffer amnesia and your identification, mobile phone, and money are all gone. You don't know who you are or where you live. So, you must move on and adapt. You now strive to make a living and survive in life the best you can. You are out in the cold working and sleeping rough every day and around some people who are friendly and others who try to take from you. Life is enjoyable sometimes, but much of the time it is a struggle, and it can be very hard at times. You observe that some people around you have horrendously difficult lives.

After a few years, someone recognizes you and takes you on a journey through the cold streets and eventually arriving at a front door of a somewhat familiar house. The front door is opened, and you are ushered in. You see a big loving family there all gathered around a table and happily enjoying each other's company. When they see you, you instantly feel this immense love and warmth radiating all over you.

Photo credit: Roman Samborskyi on Shutterstock

They all jump up, rush over to you, and welcome you home. They tell you they'd missed you and say that you must stay. Their faces seem so familiar, and a hint of your memories start to return. It feels wonderful that they know you. You realise you are home and that you have this sense that you've known these people and this place for a very long time, far longer than you've lived in the city center. Later, you look out the front window into the icy cold street. Only now, you realise how cold you were outside, but you are now back where you belong.

Well, mom, this hopefully gives you a glimpse into what it is like crossing over, but the experience will be far better than I can describe here with words. You won't remember leaving but you will be overjoyed when you return home. You'll be amazed and will wonder what it was that you liked about life back in the world.

This is not to say that you should wish for death since that's another form of attachment. But, when I was beyond, there was initially little-or-no desire to return to this world until I had the epiphanies. That people largely don't realise about this world beyond, and that people are focused on the mind/body instead of putting their focus on the spirit within. I had this sense of purpose and duty to return to the world to share what I had experienced and what lies beyond. Obviously, this book you are now reading is this aim materializing!

Preamble to mom's response

Mom, this chapter was a variety of thoughts and reflections. I think you found this one challenging since it is a collection of different ideas, but it was a pleasure to hear that you really enjoyed it. Mom, your comments are below.

Mom's response to the Cheese Course

I found it incredible that you were able to gather so much from beyond. I find that when I'm in an unfamiliar place then I have difficulty. It really was a wow moment to hear about the spirits all connecting and experiencing together, breath-taking. You are probably right that what you saw may have been the bare bones of what was beyond rather than something just created for you to make you feel comfortable there.

I have no problem with shedding the body, but you do make it sound like it could be hard to. I was pleased to hear from our discussion that I don't have to shed the body myself, that it will happen automatically. I just have to be comfortable with it being gone. You know when you are ready, 100%, that's all there is to it!

I particularly enjoyed hearing about that story of going off in the cold, windy city and that dying was like returning home to find such a warm and loving environment with family around. That felt like a light bulb moment for me, and I can imagine seeing my family waiting there in spirit form.

I raised the concern that people with a young family reading this book may be concerned if they had to be comfortable with leaving their family behind in the world. It would be difficult to convince them that the world didn't matter, and I thought that they would be thinking of their family the whole time. You mentioned that it would be difficult, but it was convincing when you explained that it was just a short experience being in this world and that nobody actually disappeared. That when you were beyond, it was like you were returning to everyone aside from those in this short experience of the world. And that eventually you all return to the spirit world beyond.

It will be a challenge to get that across, but I understand and see what you mean. I have a lot to think about from this course. It is lovely that you have written this book and are sharing it with others to help them on their journey.

DESSERT COURSE

Mom, it's now time to return to that key question raised in the palate cleanser course. Why do innocent young kids die every day of illnesses such as leukemia if there is a fair and loving God? This is such an important question to consider if we are to fully understand the world we live in and how there can be a world beyond. Obviously, this question can be broadened much more to the general reader as 'why do bad things happen to good people in this world if there exists a fair and loving God?' Enjoy this course, mom.

As mentioned from my near-death experience, right before my spirit returned to my body trapped underwater, I overheard a communication from an assisting spirit reporting that my body might not be usable anymore. The message was passed discreetly but with some concern to the spirit-in-the-light communicating with me. It may seem insignificant on the face of it, aside from adding a little urgency to the situation! In fact, it was an absolutely profound statement! Let me explain why. It told me that the spirit world was powerless to save my body dying back in the water. That meant that the spirit world does not have direct influence over this world we live in! It meant that the spirit world could return my spirit to the body only if the body was still viable. (In this book, I need a simple way to refer to this message from the assisting spirit that 'my body may not be useable', so I will refer to it as the profound statement).

It was clear, the spirit world could not repair or otherwise fix my body if the physical damage done to it was too much. Too often, people incorrectly assume that God can fix everything or do anything in this world if He wants to.

There is the assumption that if you pray hard enough or are worthy enough then God will take care of you. To me, the assisting spirit's profound statement makes the case that God does not have control or any significant influence over this world we live in. Perhaps God could have created a world in which only good things happened, but it is my impression that to make such a world then it would require knowing all its evolution right from the start and for all time in order to be sure. God would also have to know everything that we would do in our lives, how we would interpret things, and what actions we would take. That would require Him knowing everything about us and our evolution as well.

I don't think God has this as His aim, to create us and our environment to be completely predictable. On the other hand, if God wants us to evolve independent of him then the consequence is that the world becomes an unpredictable place where bad things can happen to good people, and vice versa. Assuming the above to be true, then at least there is a very pleasant conclusion from all this. If God is not affecting this world directly then it is plausible that God can have the attributes of being fair and loving, consistent with my near-death experience beyond.

So, if God didn't create the world to only have good outcomes, and doesn't fully control the world or us, then consequently the world could exist with all manner of injustices and yet there be a fair and loving God apart from it all. We are, however, left with the question as to why the world would be created to evolve independently of God? Additionally, we might also ask whether He created the world?

People get frustrated if God doesn't act to help them when bad things happen to them, but from the above, I conclude that God isn't able to act in this world and at the same time achieve the aim He has for us in this worldly experience. Very worrisome is that many young people have either never had a belief in God or lost belief along the way. To many of those people, God's inaction in this world is evidence that He doesn't exist. Consequently, many people don't even believe in any spiritual world or any continuation of themselves after death.

So, based on the profound statement that 'the body may not be usable', I conclude that God is not able to act directly in this world. I will soon outline why I believe God must be almost completely hands-off, but before I do that, I would like to mention a few ways that God (or more likely the spirit world) does interact with us. From my experience, the spirit world can influence our world in very minor ways, but mostly refrains from doing so as much as possible (or can only interact in such subtle ways that are mostly unnoticed).

One way that God or the spirit world can interact with you is through messages that appear as thoughts. Messages sent in this way are usually rare, however, but maybe prayer can encourage them. Also, perhaps prayer makes you more aware of the messages that are being received because you expect them. Whether a person who receives a message from beyond can recognize that it is from beyond depends on how spiritually receptive they are. These thoughts from beyond can easily be confused with regular thoughts, though. They are subtle since the intention is not to constrain or control your life but perhaps communicate something important at a key time.

With regards to connecting with God or the world beyond, I believe Jesus was exceptional, but he still sometimes went off from the group to communicate and receive those messages. For the rest of us, recognising a message from beyond depends crucially on how obscured our mind is with thoughts, desires, and emotions. This will determine if a message gets any traction with you at all. Obscurations can easily overwhelm these very subtle and potentially rare messages from beyond. Traditional communities sometimes culturally 'set the stage' with rituals so that individuals are more receptive to these messages.

I expect that, frequently, a person may receive a message and not even realise it is from the spirit realm. It can easily merge with your own thoughts and might influence other thoughts or actions. I really must stress that I believe these messages to be rare indeed and the spirit world really doesn't want to influence you too often, if at all. But I have recognized these subtle messages very clearly several times spread over decades.

Certainly, one example was when my spirit was returned to my body in the water whilst drowning and I received the instructions on how to escape. The channel was very clear, but I would point out that I was particularly open and receptive! The two messages that came through had commonalities in the way they arrived in my mind. As described previously, I became aware they were being sent and it was like they were bubbling up through a barrier. However, they were very subtle, and it would have been very difficult for someone to notice them if any obscurations were present at all.

Another key time was when my dad died, and his spirit was leaving the world. The messages from beyond were very clear to me then, too. There have been several other times as well, but perhaps I'll leave those for another discussion. The key point is that influences from the spirit world beyond (or God) are very subtle and likely rare, at least in my experience. So, it is clear to me that the spirit world and God are essentially not influencing you very much in this world.

As an aside, both the spirit world and our world are forced to cross paths at the start and end of our lives. When my life was ending, the spirit realm clearly dictated whether crossing was an option. That decision was not mine to make, but whether I took that option *was* my decision. So, the spirit world decides whether transitions from our world to the spirit world can take place.

I would also expect that the spirit world would decide which body would be chosen for a spirit to begin a life with, but this is merely conjecture. There is a lot of depth in this area that I'm glossing over, such as deep matters like the world evolution would therefore have to dictate the number of spirits that could be given an opportunity to experience this world, rather than the other way around, which is usually expected.

God may be hands-off (unable to act) in this world, but that doesn't exclude Him from creating the world in the first place. It is very plausible that the big bang was initiated from the spirit world or God himself. Since then, our world has followed a path largely unaffected by the spirit world/God and will continue to do so until it ceases to provide a suitable environment or collapses back in upon itself. Perhaps when the world is of no use anymore, then God might exercise full powerfulness at that stage and shut the world down, if that is possible.

Mistakenly, people think that God influences everything in this world behind the scenes. Believing this leads to all those avenues of thought that we discussed earlier including rationalizations like God works in mysterious ways, punishing karma, God likes some people more than others, God is testing your faith, etc.

Based on the evidence and experiences I've had; I don't believe God intervenes in this world aside from in minor ways. If you believe this, then it begs the question of why not? Answering this question isn't strictly necessary, but let's explore this a little further since it can provide meaning for us. Addressing it will certainly require a fair bit of conjecture, though.

The world has undergone a hugely complex and intricate evolution since the big bang. It has taken an extremely long time to get to a stage when animals exist and, much later, humans appeared. Perhaps the world had to be created and developed in this long evolution in order to be independent from God. In this way, the creatures that developed, such as us humans, would be complex enough and independent. Essentially, we would develop to be unpredictable and have some measure of free-will if God wasn't constantly monitoring and controlling our evolution. So, God must be hands-off to enable us to generate independence from Him and have that measure of unpredictable nature.

I will refrain from explicitly requiring free-will since it is a hotly contested topic. Whether we gain free-will or not is up for debate but a world that fosters unpredictable humans is enough for the discussion here. With regards to free-will, I personally tend to believe that the consciousness, and hence spirit awareness, has some sort of input into the decision-making process in terms of adding 'weightings of importance' to choices, so I do believe in a degree of free-will.

The final decision with most choices is likely made by the subconscious which can effectively weigh all the multiple factors involved in important decisions. If the decision is not very important, then likely no input from the conscious is necessary. A world in which the conscious had to make all the decisions would be an onerous one. Conversely, a world in which the body took wholly independent decisions would be a potentially frightening one. Such a world would not encourage the development of identity within.

I believe the subconscious is always checking with the conscious about 'importance weightings' regarding significant decisions. In this way, there is an element of free-will. The choices may be heavily constrained but there is scope for limited free-will, which could later blossom in a different environment, e.g., the spiritual world.

Thus, this provides the reason, raised earlier, as to why God would create the world and not constrain it to be only good. It is necessary to establish hosts for spirits that are independent and to some degree unpredictable. God must be hands-off if he wants us and our spirits to develop in a way that is independent of Him. That is, to have a degree of unpredictability and even have an element of free-will, if that is permissible. He, and we, must therefore accept the world's evolution for better or worse if that is the aim. He can't control the outcome to only be good if he wants this aim. I will refrain from suggesting free-will in future discussions and will refer to 'independent' and 'unpredictable' behavior so as not to distract the reader. Free-will is not strictly necessary but is desirable.

Why would God want us to have independence and be unpredictable? My belief is that creating some degree of unpredictability and independence in humans, and hence the spirit within them, is very desirable for God and the spirit world in general. Think about it for a moment, if you were God and were all-knowing and all-seeing (amongst many other attributes), then what would be of any interest to you anymore? Probably nothing if everything was predictable. But if humans, and the spirits attached to them, could learn actions and behaviors that were independent of God (or even take their own actions and think their own thoughts), then I'd imagine that the spirits developed in that environment would add something unique to the spirit world and for God when they returned beyond.

Whilst we are on the topic of spirits and the world. Is it possible that other creatures in this world could host a spirit as well? Obviously, I don't know for sure, but it seems very plausible, and I could think of a few animals that might be hosting spirits if it is possible.

What are the consequences of such a world designed to foster independence? Well, the world evolves purely governed by a set of physical laws that may have initially been established by God, but now this many-bodied complex evolution is well beyond what is completely predictable. Thus, in such a world, there will be all manner of unpredictable things that will happen because the world is freely evolving based on the physical governing forces and nothing else.

With no oversight from God, the evolution won't necessarily always be good, by design, for the creatures in it. This world will fast become unpredictable and the humans developing in its environment will be unpredictable too, even by God. You can't have independent development without freedom. Therefore, all manner of things can take place in such a world. But consequently, the people within it are left trying to make sense of why these things are happening, especially if they believe in a fair and loving God controlling it all. However, this world operates ungoverned and without God imposing moral oversight, by necessity.

So, you either control everything in this world (and no independence and no unpredictability of those in it) or you let the world run its course and let independence and unpredictability operate. You see, the cost of creating independent people with potentially a degree of free-will, and importantly the same for the spirits within the people, is that you bring about unpredictable behaviors in this world and hence the creation of good and bad. Consequently, things will happen that are undesirable like diseases, health conditions, and all manner of bad things.

Mom, I know you have suffered for years with a health condition. Well, it is hopefully clear from the above arguments that God is clearly not punishing you. More generally, all the ailments, tragedies, and other terrible life circumstances are not a result of God acting against people, nor punishing them in any way. It is the cost of this world generating an independent nature in humans (and their spirit's) during their time here.

This allows us to understand and answer the question raised in the Palate Cleanser course of 'why do innocent young kids die every day from illnesses such as leukemia if there is a fair and loving God?' This is the most extreme example, so the scope of the question covers more generally why bad things happen to good people if there is a fair and loving God? I trust you will understand my stance now.

Leukemia in children, and the myriad of other injustices that take place in this world, is a consequence of the physical laws governing the world's evolution and a God that is necessarily hands-off. For this world to enable independent and unpredictable people to exist and the same for their spirits, then, consequently, God must be hands-off to enable this to happen.

Why is an independent and unpredictable nature so important? More important than having a kind environment for everyone to live in? Well, the independent and unpredictable nature in this world is the key element in the process that forges the birth of the identity of the spirit within you, so it is crucial.

The injustices in this world, however, do not preclude a fair and loving God or spirit world from existing, which is consistent with my near-death experience beyond. I would hope this is some consolation for those afflicted by tragedies, that at least the spirit world and God is fair and loving and is not intending these tragedies. It is the consequence of the birth of our spirit's independence.

It was clear in my near-death experience that the spirit world does not directly control our physical world, and this explains the reason why the world appears to be a complex mixture of beauty and dread. It makes sense out of a world that can be very harsh. A world that can lead to kids dying of leukemia, as well as all manner of other miserable things that happen to good people. It is all understandable if God doesn't directly control the outcomes in this physical world. This viewpoint doesn't change those things happening, but it can change your perception of them taking place.

There is no doubt that the death of a child to illness is the worst thing that can happen to a child and their parents or guardians/carers. But, as horrendous and world-destroying as it must be, death is not nearly as devastating if it is not final and that diamond spirit within progresses forwards after the death of the body. The loss for the family and friends will be unimaginable but it is because they think the child will not exist anymore.

Take solace that God being hands-off in letting this world evolve, in turn, provides the necessary conditions for all of us to gain an independent and unpredictable spirit, including those that die young. In time, we will all be together in the spirit realm. If we focus on our 'spirit within' rather than the mind/body, then the good and bad of this world are very short-lived and affect only the physical in this world. What is crucial is that people do not view God as punishing or victimizing them or the ones they care about, since it isn't like that. Rest assured, though, that there is a fair and loving God in the spirit realm.

From my own experience, our first child tragically miscarried. This happens to more people than you might think which became clear once we eventually started talking to people about it. It was horrendously difficult at the time, and we felt a huge loss that we didn't get to meet that beautiful spirit, but I look back on it now with only positive feelings. I trust that the spirit had another opportunity to experience the world and will come to realise its own nature and independence, or maybe it was ready to cross over right there and then. I certainly look forward to meeting that little diamond spirit in the future one day.

Preamble to mom's response

This has been a very heavy course to read. It all revolved around one comment made by an assisting spirit that gave rise to a lot of thoughts about our world and God. I've immensely enjoyed our chat about all this. It has been challenging but certainly very enjoyable and worthwhile. Mom, your comments about this course are below.

Mom's response to the Dessert Course

That's really good how you recognized the importance of that comment by the assisting spirit. That would have startled and concerned me if I had overheard that. What you said about God stepping back from the world to let it run its course is an eye-opener. You laid it all out. I loved how you explained it was a trade-off, that God stands back to give our spirits their independence. It makes things simple to understand. God doesn't have to work in mysterious ways, and it explains how the world can be good and bad, and work out for some and not for others.

We had a lovely discussion about what God would do with His time, what He thought of people and whether you'd meet your parents and siblings in the spirit world. You said that you would expect my family would be there when I crossed over since all the spirits beyond who communicated with you felt like family, but since nobody in the family had died at that stage then you wouldn't have known them.

It was lovely to hear that all the spirits felt like family for long before your experience in this world! I understand that you don't have proof that I will be with my family, but it was reassuring that everyone felt like family. That is what everyone is wondering. You are so spiritual, and it is wonderful. Some people may struggle to understand some of this, but it is a gift that you should definitely share.

MIGNARDISE COURSE

Mom, I hope you'll find this to be a sweet course filled with things that make your life more peaceful. Enjoy!

One of the things I want you to know is that the spirits

Photo credit: Mariia Boiko on Shutterstock

in the world beyond create an environment that is very pleasing and comforting for those who cross over. It may not be pleasing, though, until a person releases their attachment to the mind/body, but once you are in the spirit realm it will be pleasant and completely painless.

The realm that you'll enter will be tailored to bring you comfort. I can only guess what it will be like for you, mom, but I would expect that at some point you'll experience that all-encompassing, all-pervading, loving white light through every inch of your spirit. It will be an amazing feeling of love and warmth which is incredible to experience and is very likely the Holy Spirit or God. I would also expect that you'll recognize the spirits of all your loving family and friends, and that will further ease your crossing. I trust you will have a unique and inviting experience welcoming you back one day, and just keep in mind that the spirit world will adjust the experience, like it did for me, to make you feel completely comfortable.

Now, after all this discussion of the past courses, you might be wondering, did I see God? This is a difficult question to answer with certainty. Nobody claimed to me that they were God; however, the white light was incredible, and it felt like it was the outflowing from the source of the spirit realm which I would expect was God. If there is a God, then I'd expect this white light to be Him or emanating from Him.

Alternatively, it is possible that the spirit-in-the-light was God speaking to me from within the light. I would point out that I didn't look fully into the light as I knew that was the point at which I would have certainly crossed over and left this world permanently. From the Bible, some readers may associate the spirit-in-the-light with a gatekeeper since the spirit was at the 'entrance' to crossing over. Perhaps, but I want to make it clear that I didn't feel like there was any judgement taking place in that traditional sense, so that doesn't exactly fit.

Perhaps meeting God only occurs after you cross over. I wouldn't have thought that God would have a form like us or maybe any form at all, so it is very possible that I did experience God. He could probably exhibit any form, if needed, to make us feel comfortable. Alternatively, if there is only a spirit realm and no God, then the white light must have been some sort of manifestation of the essence of that spirit world. It certainly felt heavenly to be within that light and I'd say that I was experiencing God or as close as one could get to Him without passing.

You might be wondering what the spirits looked like, at least the ones that I could see clearly. They are very difficult to describe and maybe I shouldn't attempt this because we don't come across this sort of form in the world. So, keep in mind that any description will be very approximate and might mislead you, but here goes.

The spirits had a discernible form, but not like a usual body. They were more like an energy form. Each individual spirit appeared like a sparkler, but without the sparks flying off and with far more depth and complexity. Don't take this comparison too seriously since the spirits weren't hot or anything like that, but they did look like vibrant energy forms. You can imagine them as an illuminated diamond with energy emanating from them, if you like, but not emanating like the white light I described earlier.

The spirits appeared to be pure and, interestingly, they could give you a feel about their past in the world. They did this by exhibiting what can be described as traits about their past experiences. These traits, and the way a spirit communicated, were the ways you could potentially recognize a spirit as someone you may have known previously in the world. These traits weren't evident all the time, though, but they were especially apparent when a spirit communicated. They could somehow give you a feel of their history from their time in the world.

Who a spirit was back in the world didn't seem to matter too much now, though, but it did make everything more comfortable for me during my experience. I felt like I really should have known many of the individual spirits who communicated with me, but I didn't. This bothered me for some time afterwards. It was one of the factors preventing me from later talking about the experience. But, as mentioned, I didn't know anyone close who had died by that time, so it was not surprising. It has made me think much more about seeking to connect with people in this world at a deeper spiritual level now, since it may be useful when you are beyond. The spirits felt very much like family and like they had been so for a very long time, well before I had had the worldly experience.

The spirit-in-the-light was different in authority to

the other spirits, though, and had an important role. Unfortunately, I didn't get to see the worldly traits of that spirit, though. Mom, I know you have your roots in Christianity from your upbringing. Rest assured that everything I experienced was completely consistent with what I'd consider to be the stripped back teachings of Christianity.

Mom, you should view dying as somewhat sad as you will be saying goodbye to your body, but the whole essence of you will not disappear. Bid goodbye to the body like a boat transporting you to another shore. Walk onto that shore and treat it as an adventure, and you may end up in another body being born again or you may be given the opportunity to cross over. As mentioned, one of the beautiful things I found in the spirit world is that the experience is designed to put you at ease. Be open, trust, and expect the spirit world to guide you through the transition in such a way that makes you feel safe, loved, and welcomed.

How should you prepare for dying? A lot could be said on this topic, but most importantly, be ready to relinquish the mind/body and reside in what has been familiar to you all your life. That familiar part of you that is the quiet, unchanging 'you' in the background of everything and underneath the mind obscurations that partly cloud that diamond spirit within.

Preamble to mom's response

You liked the sound of the Dessert Course right from the start! It really is a pleasant course with straight-forward messages and a joy to read to you. As we now come towards the end of the book, I was thrilled to hear that it has really put your mind at ease about death. I have certainly satisfied the main purpose of writing this book when I heard that. As always, I've really enjoyed our chats about all of this. Mom, a summary of your comments from our discussion is below.

Mom's response to the Mignardise Course

Hearing about all of this has lifted my worries of passing. Like you said, I will expect to experience something that is appropriate for me. It sounds so beautiful and gives me a warm feeling just discussing it. You mentioned about whether you met God. I really believe you did. It's fine if I'm not correct, no harm done, but that's what I feel.

We had a good discussion about what might happen if the body died, and I wasn't ready to cross. That your spirit may go into a new life if it isn't ready to cross. For me, it doesn't need to be clear cut as to what will happen, but I now expect a pleasant experience without judgements and that eases my mind. To be welcomed by the spirits of my family would be everything.

COFFEE OR BRANDY DIGESTIFS

Sadly, we have reached the last course. It has been a marvelous time sharing and discussing these experiences with you and bringing you greater peace in your later years. I've immensely enjoyed our evening talks on the telephone bridging the two continents that separate us. You, ensuring at least one hearing aid was in, or we'd end up in the most amusing conversations! Me, balancing a pillow on my shoulder to support my phone as I took notes from our discussions! We've made it work! It has given us so much to talk about and share and that has been wonderful. Well, onwards to our last course. I am sure you will enjoy this one, mom.

Mom, you are loved, and when death comes your way, like it did for me, then embrace that you are loved in this world and let go if you know the time is right to pass. You will instinctively know. As it is happening,

reside in your spirit awareness and be open to what comes and develops in this adventure of a lifetime. I am sure it will be a warm and loving welcome from familiar spirits looking forward to being with you again and eager for you to join them. Just know that when you experience that white light, you will experience unimaginable love and completeness.

Photo credit: author

If everything feels right, then put the world behind you and move forwards in this adventure. I imagine that the spirit world will have done their homework and there will be lovely hanging planters full of beautiful flowers either side of the white light when you are encouraged to cross over! I hope you have a beautiful experience transitioning beyond and you'll reunite with your loving family and many more familiar spirits. If my time comes after yours then I'll be looking forward to seeing you there beyond!

This little book has been a lifetime in the making and it gives me great pleasure to think all the way back to when I was being comforted by you as a child dealing with my fear of death. I was fearful of what was going to happen, but that is in the past now and resolved. I hope this book, full of my experiences and thoughts, provides you in return with comfort about what to expect in the distant future when your time does come. Mom, expect an incredible and enjoyable adventure, and we will all meet up again—beyond—in the future one day.

Preamble to mom's response

Writing this book for you and then reading and discussing it with you has been one of the best experiences of my life. I will keep my promise to get it published so that you can see and hold a printed copy and know that it is reaching others. I know it has taken years to create and refine, but it has been an immense pleasure to discuss it with you.

The overarching satisfaction I take from writing this book is to hear that it has completely eased your worries and allowed you to know that you will continue beyond when the time comes. Rest assured, it will be a beautiful experience transitioning beyond this world. I've enjoyed our long discussions and I'll end this book the way we end every call with, 'I love you'. Mom, your final comments are listed below.

Mom's response to Coffee or Brandy Digestifs

This course was so sweet. I loved all the lovely words you said and feel so lucky. It has been a wonderful experience and I've enjoyed all the attention! I love the book! It has given me a lot of knowledge and great confidence about what is to come. It has made me feel safe knowing what to expect. It's like I'm floating with a big weight off my shoulders. It wasn't worrying me too much, but it really is lovely to have everything clarified for me. Yes, when you cross, I'll be on the welcoming committee! How's that! I loved your last sentence—it touched my heart and I love you too.

Mom, keep on smiling and enjoying life!

Photo credit: author

Love you, mom

Your son

ABOUT THE AUTHOR

The author was raised in both the UK and Canada. He earned a B.Sc. in physics from the University of Toronto and M.Sc. and Ph.D. degrees in physics from Dalhousie University. The author currently lives in Yorkshire, England with his wife and three children. His passions are family, developing barista skills, and hiking in the Yorkshire Dales and the Lake District.

RELATED WORKS

The author is developing a journal for the reader to record their personal thoughts and memories for a loved one, like the author did for his mother in this book. It is a guided journal with a series of important questions and provides space for your heartfelt responses. Complete it and give it to a chosen loved one, whether it be your mom, dad, or another special person. To obtain the journal and to read more about the author, please visit:

www.sharingheavenwithmom.org

Book cover: the composite graphic was developed by the author. For the front cover, credit is given for the use of the Shutterstock stock photo ID 1540652960 by Wirestock Creators. For the back cover, photo credit for the image is attributed to the author.

Printed in Great Britain
by Amazon